CW00551252

Spanish Dialogues for Beginners
Book 2

Book 2

Over 100 Daily Used Phrases and Short Stories to Learn Spanish in Your Car. Have Fun and Grow Your Vocabulary with Crazy Effective Language Learning Lessons

LEARN LIKE A NATIVE

www.LearnLikeNatives.com

© **Copyright 2021**

By Learn Like A Native

ALL RIGHTS RESERVED

TABLE OF CONTENT

www.LearnLikeNatives.com

INTRODUCTION

Before we dive into some Spanish, I want to congratulate you, whether you're just beginning, continuing, or resuming your language learning journey. Here at Learn Like a Native, we understand the determination it takes to pick up a new language and after reading this book, you'll be another step closer to achieving your language goals.

As a thank you for learning with us, we are giving you free access to our 'Speak Like a Native' eBook. It's packed full of practical advice and insider tips on how to make language learning quick, easy, and most importantly, enjoyable. Head over to LearnLikeNatives.com to access your free guide and peruse our huge selection of language learning resources.

Learning a new language is a bit like cooking—you need several different ingredients and the right technique, but the end result is sure to be delicious. We created this book of short stories for learning Spanish because language is alive. Language is about the senses—hearing, tasting the words on your tongue, and touching another culture up close. Learning a language in a classroom is a fine place to start, but it's not a complete introduction to a language.

In this book, you'll find a language come to life. These short stories are miniature immersions into the Spanish language, at a level that is perfect for beginners. This book is not a lecture on grammar. It's not an endless vocabulary list. This book is the closest you can come to a language immersion without leaving the country. In the stories within, you will see people speaking to each other, going through daily life situations, and using the most common, helpful words and phrases in language.

You are holding the key to bringing your Spanish studies to life.

Made for Beginners

We made this book with beginners in mind. You'll find that the language is simple, but not boring. Most of the book is in the present tense, so you will be able to focus on dialogues, root verbs, and understand and find patterns in subject-verb agreement.

This is not "just" a translated book. While reading novels and short stories translated into Spanish is a wonderful thing, beginners (and even novices) often run into difficulty. Literary licenses and complex sentence structure can make reading in your second language truly difficult—not to mention BORING. That's why Spanish Short

Stories for Beginners is the perfect book to pick up. The stories are simple, but not infantile. They were not written for children, but the language is simple so that beginners can pick it up.

The Benefits of Learning a Second Language

If you have picked up this book, it's likely that you are already aware of the many benefits of learning a second language. Besides just being fun, knowing more than one language opens up a whole new world to you. You will be able to communicate with a much larger chunk of the world. Opportunities in the workforce will open up, and maybe even your day-to-day work will be improved. Improved communication can also help you expand your business. And from a neurological perspective, learning a second language is like taking your daily vitamins and eating well, for your brain!

How To Use The Book

The chapters of this book all follow the same structure:

- A short story with several dialogs
- A summary in Spanish
- A list of important words and phrases and their English translation
- Questions to test your understanding
- Answers to check if you were right
- The English translation of the story to clear every doubt

You may use this book however is comfortable for you, but we have a few recommendations for getting the most out of the experience. Try these tips and if they work for you, you can use them on every chapter throughout the book.

1) Start by reading the story all the way through. Don't stop or get hung up on any particular words or phrases. See how much of the plot you can understand in this way. We think you'll get a lot more of it than you may expect, but it is completely normal not to understand everything in the story. You are learning a new language, and that takes time.

2) Read the summary in Spanish. See if it matches what you have understood of the plot.

3) Read the story through again, slower this time. See if you can pick up the meaning of any words or phrases you don't understand by using context clues and the information from the summary.

4) Test yourself! Try to answer the five comprehension questions that come at the end of each story. Write your answers down, and then check them against the answer key. How did you do? If you didn't get them all, no worries!

5) Look over the vocabulary list that accompanies the chapter. Are any of these the words you did not understand? Did you already know the meaning of some of them from your reading?

6) Now go through the story once more. Pay attention this time to the words and phrases you haven't understand. If you'd like, take the time to look them up to

expand your meaning of the story. Every time you read over the story, you'll understand more and more.

7) Move on to the next chapter when you are ready.

Read and Listen

The audio version is the best way to experience this book, as you will hear a native Spanish speaker tell you each story. You will become accustomed to their accent as you listen along, a huge plus for when you want to apply your new language skills in the real world.

If this has ignited your language learning passion and you are keen to find out what other resources are available, go to **LearnLikeNatives.com**, where you can access our vast range of free learning materials. Don't know where to begin? An excellent place to start is our 'Speak Like a Native' free eBook, full of practical advice and insider tips on how to make language learning quick, easy, and most importantly, enjoyable.

And remember, small steps add up to great advancements! No moment is better to begin learning than the present.

FREE BOOK!

Get the *FREE BOOK* that reveals the
secrets path to learn any language fast,
and without leaving your country.

Discover:

- The **language 5 golden rules** to
  master languages at will

- Proven **mind training techniques** to
  revolutionize your learning

- A complete step-by-step guide to
  conquering any language

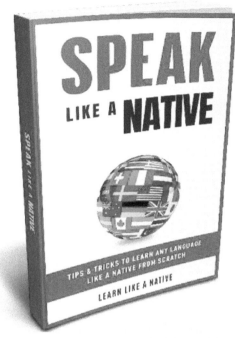

CHAPTER 1
John's Homework / School
+ Classroom

HISTORIA

L a Sra. Kloss es una **maestra** de cuarto grado. Enseña en la Escuela Primaria Homewood. La **escuela** está en un edificio de ladrillos rojo. Queda en un pueblo pequeño.

La Sra. Kloss tiene una **clase** de 15 estudiantes. Sus **estudiantes** son niños y niñas. Generalmente son buenos estudiantes. La Sra. Kloss tiene una rutina. Sus estudiantes empiezan el día en sus **escritorios**, sentados en sus **sillas**. La Sra. Kloss **pasa lista**.

"¿Louise?", dice ella.

"¡Aquí!" grita Louise.

"¿Mike?" dice la Sra. Kloss.

"Presente", dice Mike.

"¿John?"

"Aquí, Sra. Kloss", dice John.

Y así sucesivamente. Después de pasar lista, la Sra. Kloss comienza el día con **matemáticas**. Para sus estudiantes, las matemáticas son difíciles. La clase escucha a la Sra. Kloss enseñar. Observan como escribe en la **pizarra**. A veces, un estudiante resuelve un problema frente a la clase. Usan **tiza** para escribir la solución. Los otros estudiantes hacen los problemas en sus **cuadernos**.

El momento favorito de todos es el almuerzo. La clase va al comedor. Tienen dos opciones. Una opción es una comida saludable de carne y verduras. La otra opción es pizza o hamburguesas. Algunos estudiantes traen un almuerzo de casa.

Por la tarde, estudian **historia**. Los viernes, tienen clase de ciencias en el laboratorio. Hacen **experimentos**, como cultivar plantas de un pedazo de papa.

La Sra. Kloss les da a sus estudiantes **tarea** todos los días. Se llevan el trabajo a casa. Trabajan de noche. Al día siguiente, lo traen a la escuela. La única excusa para los deberes incompletos es una nota de sus padres.

Un día, la clase revisa los deberes de **inglés** juntos.

"Todos, por favor traigan sus **papeles** a mi escritorio", dice la Sra. Kloss. Todos llevan sus tareas a la Sra. Kloss. Todos excepto John.

"John, ¿dónde está tu tarea?" dice la Sra. Kloss.

La cara de John está muy roja. Está nervioso.

"No lo tengo", dice John.

"¿Tiene una nota de sus padres?", pregunta la Sra. Kloss.

"No", dice John.

"¿Por qué no hiciste tu tarea, entonces?" pregunta la Sra. Kloss. John dice algo muy calladamente.

"¿Qué? No podemos oírte", dice la Sra. Kloss. Ella le da a John una sonrisa amable. Parece nervioso.

"Mi perro se comió mi tarea", dice John. La Sra. Kloss y los otros estudiantes se ríen. Esta excusa es la excusa más típica cuando no han hecho el trabajo.

"¿Está en tu **mochila**? ¿O quizás en tu **casillero**?" pregunta la Sra. Kloss. Quiere ayudar a John.

"¡No, mi perro se lo comió!" insiste John.

"Esa es la **excusa más vieja del libro**", dice la Sra. Kloss.

"¡Es verdad!", dice John.   John es un buen estudiante. Normalmente **saca A**. La Sra. Kloss no quiere enviar a Jon a la **oficina del director** por mentir. No le cree a John, pero decide darle otra oportunidad.

"Traiga la tarea mañana", dice la Sra. Kloss. "Aquí tiene otra copia". John toma la **hoja de trabajo** y agradece a la Sra. Kloss. La clase saca su cuaderno de **arte**. Hoy en clase de arte están dibujando con **lápices** de colores. Los estudiantes aman las clases de arte. Es una oportunidad para relajarse. Dibujan y dibujan hasta que suena la **campana**. La escuela ha terminado.

Los estudiantes hablan en los pasillos. Intercambian notas. Los estudiantes de cuarto grado esperan afuera. Sus padres los recogen. Algunos de ellos se van a pie. Algunos de ellos se van en coches. Los profesores les ayudan a encontrar a sus padres.

La Sra. Kloss termina su trabajo. Empaca su **laptop** en su bolsa. Su aula está limpia y vacía. Sale a la calle. Mientras camina hacia su auto, ve a John y a su papá. El padre de John lo recoge con su perro. La Sra. Kloss saluda a John y a su padre.

"¡Hola, John!" dice la Sra. Kloss.

"Buenas tardes, Sra. Kloss", dice John.

"¿Este es el perro que se comió tu tarea?" pregunta la Sra. Kloss. Ella sonríe, así que John sabe que está bromeando.

"Sí, Sra. Kloss", dice el padre de John. "Gracias por entender. ¡John está tan preocupado por meterse en problemas!"

¡La Sra. Kloss está conmocionada! Esta vez, el perro realmente se comió la tarea.

Lista de Vocabulario

teacher	profesor / profesora
school	escuela
class	clase
students	estudiantes
desk	escritorio
chair	silla
roll call	pasar lista
math	matemáticas
blackboard	pizarra
chalk	tiza
notebook	cuaderno
history	historia
science	ciencia
lab	laboratorio
experiment	experimento

homework	tarea
English	inglés
papers	papeles
backpack	mochila
locker	casillero
the oldest excuse in the book	la excusa más antigua del libro
straight A's	sobresaliente
principal's office	oficina del director
worksheet	hoja de trabajo
pencils	lápices
bell	campana
laptop	laptop

PREGUNTAS

1) ¿Cómo comienza el día en la clase de la Sra. Kloss?

    a) los estudiantes se ponen de pie y gritan

    b) con una tarea asignada

    c) pasando lista

    d) La Sra. Kloss grita

2) ¿Cuál es la hora favorita del día en la Escuela Primaria Homewood?

    a) pasar la lista

    b) hora del almuerzo

    c) clase de matemáticas

    d) después de que suena la campana

3) ¿Por qué la Sra. Kloss dice que la excusa de John es la más antigua del libro?

    a) porque todo el mundo usa esa excusa

    b) Juan es el mayor de la clase

    c) olvidó su libro

    d) su perro tiene siete años

4) ¿Qué tienes que tener si no haces tú tarea?

    a) un experimento científico

    b) una buena excusa

    c) nada, está bien

    d) una nota de tus padres

5) ¿Por qué se sorprende la Sra. Kloss al final de la historia?

    a) se da cuenta de que John estaba diciendo la verdad

b) El perro de Juan es en realidad un caballo

c) Juan no le habla

d) El padre de John se parece a John

RESPUESTAS

1) ¿Cómo comienza el día en la clase de la Sra. Kloss?

c) pasando lista

2) ¿Cuál es la hora favorita del día en la Escuela Primaria Homewood?

b) hora del almuerzo

29

3) ¿Por qué la Sra. Kloss dice que la excusa de John es la más antigua del libro?

    a) porque todo el mundo usa esa excusa

4) ¿Qué tienes que tener si no haces tú tarea?

    d) una nota de tus padres

5) ¿Por qué se sorprende la Sra. Kloss al final de la historia?

    a) se da cuenta de que John estaba diciendo la verdad

Translation of the Story

John's Homework

STORY

Mrs. Kloss is a grade 4 **teacher**. She teaches at Homewood Elementary School. The **school** is in a red brick building. It is in a small town.

Mrs. Kloss has a **class** of 15 students. Her **students** are boys and girls. They are usually good students. Mrs. Kloss has a routine. Her students start the day at their **desks**, seated in their **chairs**. Mrs. Kloss calls **roll call**.

"Louise?" she says.

"Here!" shouts Louise.

"Mike?" says Mrs. Kloss.

"Present," says Mike.

"John?"

"Here, Mrs. Kloss," John says.

And so on. After roll call, Mrs. Kloss starts the day with **math**. For her students, math is difficult. The class listens to Mrs. Kloss teach. They watch as she writes on the **blackboard**. Sometimes, one student solves a problem in front of the class. They use **chalk** to write out the solution. The other students do the problems in their **notebooks**.

Everyone's favorite time is lunch time. The class goes to the lunchroom. They have two choices. One choice is a healthy meal of meat and vegetables. The other choice is pizza or hamburgers. Some students bring a lunch from home.

In the afternoon, they study **history**. On Fridays, they have **science** class in the **lab**. They do **experiments**, like growing plants from a piece of potato.

Mrs. Kloss gives her students **homework** every day. They take the work home. They work at night. The next day, they bring it to school. The only excuse for incomplete homework is a note from their parents.

One day, the class reviews the **English** homework together.

"Everyone, please bring your **papers** to my desk," says Mrs. Kloss. Everyone brings their homework to Mrs. Kloss. Everyone except for John.

"John, where is your homework?" says Mrs. Kloss.

John's face is very red. He is nervous.

"I don't have it," says John.

"Do you have a note from your parents?" asks Mrs. Kloss.

"No," says John.

"Why didn't you do your homework, then?" asks Mrs. Kloss. John says something very quietly.

"What? We can't hear you," says Mrs. Kloss. She gives John a kind smile. He looks nervous.

"My dog ate my homework," says John. Mrs. Kloss and the other students laugh. This excuse is the most typical excuse for not having work done.

"Is it in your **backpack**? Or maybe your **locker**?" asks Mrs. Kloss. She wants to help John.

"No, my dog ate it!" insists John.

"That's the **oldest excuse in the book**," says Mrs. Kloss.

"It is true!" says John. John is a good student. He usually makes **straight A's**. Mrs. Kloss does not want to send Jon to the **principal's office** for lying. She does not believe John, but she decides to give him another chance.

"Bring the homework tomorrow," says Mrs. Kloss. "Here is another copy." John takes the **worksheet** and thanks Mrs. Kloss. The class turns to their **art** notebook. Today in art class they are drawing a picture with colored **pencils**. Students love art class. It is a chance to relax. They draw and draw until the **bell** rings. School is over.

Students talk in the hallways. They exchange notes. The Grade 4 students wait outside. Their parents pick them up. Some of them are on foot. Some of them are in cars. The teachers help them to find their parents.

Mrs. Kloss finishes her work. She packs her **laptop** into her bag. Her classroom is clean and empty. She goes outside. As she walks to her car, she see John and his dad. John's father picks him up with their dog. Mrs. Kloss waves to John and his father.

"Hello, John!" says Mrs. Kloss.

"Good afternoon, Mrs. Kloss," John says.

"Is this the dog that ate your homework?" asks Mrs. Kloss. She smiles, so John knows she is teasing.

"Yes, Mrs. Kloss," says John's father. "Thank you for understanding. John is so worried about getting in trouble!"

Mrs. Kloss is shocked! This time, the dog really did eat the homework.

CHAPTER 2
Thrift Store Bargain / house and furniture

HISTORIA

Louise y Mary son mejores amigas. También son compañeras de piso. Comparten un apartamento en el centro de la ciudad. Hoy quieren comprar muebles para su casa. Louise y Mary son estudiantes. No tienen mucho dinero.

"¿Dónde podemos comprar?", le pregunta Louise a Mary.

"Necesitamos muchos muebles", dice Mary. Le preocupa el dinero.

"Lo sé", dice Louise. "Necesitamos encontrar una **oferta**."

"Tengo una idea. ¡Vamos a la tienda de segunda mano!", dice Mary.

"¡Gran idea!", dice Louise.

Las dos chicas conducen el coche a la tienda de segunda mano. Es una tienda gigante. El edificio es más grande que diez **casas**.

Las chicas aparcan el coche. El aparcamiento está vacío.

"Vaya", dice Louise. "La tienda es muy grande."

"Totalmente", dice María. "Y no hay nadie aquí."

"Seremos las únicas personas", dice Louise. "Podemos **sentirnos como en casa**."

Las chicas entran en la tienda. La tienda lo tiene todo. A la derecha, está la sección de cocina. Hay **refrigeradores** altos y **microondas** viejos en los **estantes**. Hay **tostadoras** de todos los colores. Los precios son buenos. Un microondas cuesta solamente $10.

Todo es una oferta. Los artículos son usados y de segunda mano. Sin embargo, Mary y Louise encuentran artículos que les gustan. Hay más de una docena de sofás. Ellas necesitan un **sofá**. Pasan el tiempo hablando de los diferentes sofás.

A Mary le gusta un sofá de cuero marrón. A Louise le gusta un gran sofá púrpura. No pueden decidir. Louise ve una **silla** púrpura. Las chicas deciden adquirir el sofá y la silla púrpura para que coincidan. Es perfecto para su hogar.

"Necesito una **cama** para mi **dormitorio**", dice Louise.

Las chicas caminan a la zona del dormitorio. Primero, pasan la sección de arte.

"Ya sabes, necesitamos algo para las **paredes**", dice Louise. Mary está de acuerdo. Hay cuadros grandes, cuadros pequeños, **marcos** vacíos y fotografías en marcos. Louise decide una pintura grande y abstracta. Tiene líneas de salpicaduras de pintura roja, azul y negra.

"Puedo pintar así", dice Mary. "Parece la pintura de un niño."

41

"Son sólo cinco dólares", dice Louise.

"¡Oh, está bien!" dice Mary.

Las chicas terminan de comprar. Louise también encuentra una **lámpara** para su dormitorio. Su dormitorio es demasiado oscuro. Mary elige una **alfombra** para el **baño**. Las chicas son muy felices. Gastan sólo $ 100 dólares para todos los muebles.

"Por eso comprar en la tienda de segunda mano es una ganga", dice Louise.

"¡Sí, tenemos **todo menos el fregadero!**", dice Mary.

Mary y Louise tienen una fiesta en su apartamento esa noche. Es una fiesta para dar la bienvenida a sus amigos. Mary y Louise quieren mostrar sus nuevos muebles.

Suena el timbre. Mary abre la **puerta**. Nick es el primero en llegar. Nick es el amigo de Mary. Nick también es un estudiante. Estudia historia del arte.

"Hola, señoritas", dice Nick. "Gracias por invitarme."

"¡Entra, Nick!", dice Mary. Nick entra en el **vestíbulo**. Ella lo abraza.

"¿Quieres ver nuestras cosas nuevas?", pregunta Louise.

"¡Sí!", dice Nick.

Louise y Mary muestran a Nick el apartamento. Están contentos con la **sala de estar**. El nuevo sofá, silla y la pintura se ven muy bien.

"Todo esto es de la tienda de segunda mano", dice Mary. Está orgullosa.

Nick camina hacia la pintura. "Me gusta mucho esta pintura", dice.

"Yo también", dice Louise. "Yo la escogí."

"Me recuerda a Jackson Pollock", dice Nick.

"¿Quién es Jackson Pollock?", pregunta Mary.

"Es un pintor muy famoso", dice Nick. "Salpica pintura sobre lienzo. Igual que éste." Nick mira de cerca la pintura.

"¿Está firmado?", pregunta. Louise sacude la cabeza no. "Miremos detrás de él entonces."

Sacan la pintura del marco y la dan vuelta. Todos están tranquilos. En la parte inferior hay una firma que se parece a Jackson Pollock.

"¿Cuánto pagaste por esto?" pregunta Nick.

"Unos cinco dólares", dice Louise.

"Esto probablemente valga por lo menos $10 millones de dólares", dice Nick. Está sorprendido. Mary mira a Louise. Louise mira a Mary.

"¿Alguien quiere una copa de champán?", dice Mary.

¡Eso sí que es una ganga!

Lista de Vocabulario

roommates	compañeros de cuarto
apartment	apartamento
furniture	mueble
home	hogar
bargain	Oferta / Ganga
thrift store	tienda de segunda mano
house	casa
make ourselves at home	sentirnos como en casa
kitchen	cocina
refrigerators	refrigeradores
microwaves	microondas
shelves	estantes
toasters	tostadoras

chair	silla
table	mesa
sofa	sofá
bed	cama
bedroom	dormitorio
wall	pared
frame	marco
lamp	lámpara
carpet	alfombra
bathroom	baño
everything but the kitchen sink	todo menos el fregadero de la cocina
door	puerta
foyer	vestíbulo
living room	sala de estar

PREGUNTAS

1) ¿Por qué Mary y Louise van a la tienda de segunda mano?

    a) Ellas necesitan dinero.

    b) Necesitan muebles, pero no tienen mucho dinero.

    c) Tienen muebles que vender.

    d) Ellas quieren divertirse.

2) ¿Por qué los precios en la tienda de segunda mano son tan bajos?

    a) Es temporada de venta.

    b) Se está cerrando.

    c) Los artículos son usados.

    d) Los precios son normales, no bajos.

3) ¿Cuál de los siguientes artículos va en una cocina?

a) cama

b) microondas

c) ducha

d) sofá

4) ¿Cómo sabe Nick tanto sobre la pintura?

a) Es un comerciante de arte profesional.

b) El cuadro pertenece a Nick.

c) Estudia el arte.

d) Leyó un libro.

5) Al final, María y Luisa están...

a) tristes.

b) sorprendidas y ricas.

c) enojadas con Nick.

d) demasiado cansadas para tener una fiesta.

RESPUESTAS

1) ¿Por qué Mary y Louise van a la tienda de segunda mano?

b) Necesitan muebles, pero no tienen mucho dinero.

2) ¿Por qué los precios en la tienda de segunda mano son tan bajos?

c) Los artículos son usados.

3) ¿Cuál de los siguientes artículos va en una cocina?

b) microondas

4) ¿Cómo sabe Nick tanto sobre la pintura?

c) Estudia el arte.

5) Al final, María y Luisa están...

    b) sorprendidas y ricas.

Translation of the Story

Thrift Store Bargain

STORY

Louise and Mary are best friends. They are also **roommates**. They share an **apartment** in the center of town. Today they want to shop for **furniture** for their **home**. Louise and Mary are both students. They do not have much money.

"Where can we shop?" Louise asks Mary.

"We need a lot of furniture," Mary says. She is worried about money.

"I know," says Louise. "We need to find a **bargain**."

"I have an idea. Let's go to the thrift store!" says Mary.

"Great idea!" says Louise.

The two girls drive the car to the thrift store. It is a giant store. The building is bigger than ten **houses**.

The girls park the car. The parking lot is empty.

"Wow," says Louise. "The store is very big."

"Totally," says Mary. "And there is nobody here."

"We will be the only people," says Louise. "We can **make ourselves at home.**"

The girls walk into the store. The store has everything. On the right, there is the **kitchen** section. There are tall **refrigerators** and old **microwaves** on the **shelves**. There are **toasters** of all colors. The prices are good. A microwave costs only $10.

Everything is a bargain. The items are used and second-hand. However, Mary and Louise find items that they like. There are more than a dozen sofas. Mary and Louise need a **sofa**. They spend time talking about the different sofas. Mary likes a brown leather sofa. Louise likes a big purple sofa. They cannot decide. Louise sees a purple **chair**. The girls decide to get the purple sofa and chair so that they match. It is perfect for their home.

"I need a **bed** for my **bedroom**," says Louise.

The girls walk to the bedroom area. First, they pass the art section.

"You know, we need something for the **walls**," says Louise. Mary agrees. There are big paintings, small paintings, empty **frames**, and photographs in frames. Louise decides on a big, abstract painting. It has lines of splattered red, blue, and black paint.

"I can paint like that," says Mary. "It looks like a child's painting."

"It's only five dollars," says Louise.

"Oh, ok!" says Mary.

The girls finish shopping. Louise also finds a **lamp** for her bedroom. Her bedroom is too dark.

Mary chooses a **carpet** for the **bathroom**. The girls are very happy. They spend only $100 dollars for all the furniture.

"That is why shopping at the thrift store is a bargain," says Louise.

"Yes, we got **everything but the kitchen sink**!" says Mary.

Mary and Louise have a party in their apartment that night. It is a party to welcome friends. Mary and Louise want to show their new furniture.

The doorbell rings. Mary opens the **door**. Nick is the first to arrive. Nick is Mary's friend. Nick is also a student. He studies art history.

"Hi, ladies," says Nick. "Thank you for inviting me."

"Come in, Nick!" says Mary. Nick steps into the **foyer**. She hugs him.

"Do you want to see our new stuff?" asks Louise.

"Yeah!" says Nick.

Louise and Mary show Nick around the apartment. They are happy with the **living room**. The new sofa, chair and painting looks great.

"All of this is from the thrift store," says Mary. She is proud.

Nick walks up to the painting. "I really like this painting," he says.

"I do too," says Louise. "I chose it."

"It reminds me of Jackson Pollock," says Nick.

"Who is Jackson Pollock?" asks Mary.

"He is a very famous painter," says Nick. "He splashes paint onto canvas. Just like this one." Nick looks closely at the painting.

"Is it signed?" he asks. Louise shakes her head no. "Let's look behind it then."

They take the painting out of the frame and turn it around. They all are quiet. On the bottom is a signature that looks like 'Jackson Pollock'.

"How much did you pay for this?" asks Nick.

"About five dollars," says Louise.

"This is probably worth at least $10 million dollars," says Nick. He is shocked. Mary looks at Louise. Louise looks at Mary.

"Does anyone want a glass of champagne?" says Mary.

Now that is a bargain!

CHAPTER 3

The Goat / common present tense verbs

O llie se despierta. El sol brilla. Recuerda: es sábado. Hoy su padre no **trabaja**. Eso significa que Ollie y su padre **hacen** algo juntos. ¿Qué pueden hacer? Ollie **quiere** ir al cine. También quiere jugar videojuegos.

Ollie tiene doce años. Va a la escuela. El sábado no va a la escuela. **Usa** el sábado para hacer lo que quiera. Su padre le deja decidir. Así que Ollie quiere hacer algo divertido.

"¡Paaaaaaa!" **llama** Ollie. "¡**Ven** aquí!"

Ollie espera.

Su padre entra en la habitación de Ollie.

"Hoy es sábado", **dice** Ollie.

"Lo **sé**, hijo", dice el padre de Ollie.

"¡Quiero hacer algo divertido!", dice Ollie.

"Yo también", dice papá.

"¿Qué podemos hacer?", **pregunta** Ollie.

"¿Qué quieres hacer?", le pregunta su padre.

"Vamos al cine", dice Ollie.

"Siempre vamos al cine los sábados", dice el padre de Ollie.

"Juguemos videojuegos", dice Ollie.

"¡Jugamos videojuegos todos los días!", dice papá.

"Ok, ok", dice Ollie. Él **piensa**. Recuerda a su maestro en la escuela. Su maestro les **dice** a los estudiantes que salgan, que el aire fresco es bueno. En la escuela, ellos estudian animales. Ollie aprende acerca de los animales de la selva, los animales del océano, y los animales de las granjas.

¡Eso es, ya está!

"¡Papá, vamos a una granja!", dice Ollie. El padre de Ollie piensa que es una gran idea. Siempre ha querido **ver** y tocar animales de granja.

Toman el coche. El padre de Ollie conduce al campo. Ven un cartel que dice "Granja de animales". Siguen las indicaciones y aparcan el coche.

Ollie y su papá compran tickets para entrar. Los tickets cuestan $5. Salen de la taquilla. Hay un gran edificio de madera, la granja. Detrás de la casa de campo, hay un campo enorme. El campo tiene árboles, césped, y cercas. En cada valla hay un tipo diferente de animal. Hay cientos de animales.

Ollie está emocionado. Ve pollos, caballos, patos y cerdos. Los toca y los escucha. Ollie **hace** un sonido a cada animal. A los patos les dice "cuac". A los cerdos les dice "oink". A los caballos les dice "nay". A los pollos les dice "pio pio". Los animales miran a Ollie.

Más allá de los animales en jaulas, Ollie ve un rebaño de ovejas. El padre de Ollie le dice que las ovejas hembras se llaman ovejas. Las ovejas machos son carneros. Las ovejas bebé se llaman corderos. Las ovejas están comiendo hierba.

"Pueden vernos", dice papá.

"Pero no nos están mirando", dice Ollie.

"Las ovejas pueden ver detrás de sí mismas. No tienen que girar la cabeza", dice papá. El padre de Ollie sabe mucho sobre las ovejas.

"Cortan el pelo de las ovejas en primavera", dice papá. Le dice a Ollie cómo la lana de las ovejas se **convierte** en suéteres, bufandas y otras prendas de abrigo. Ollie tiene un suéter hecho de lana. Es cálido.

Ollie y su papá caminan por el campo. La hierba es verde. Hay vacas en una esquina. Una de las vacas madres alimenta a un ternero.

"¿Sabes lo que hacen las vacas, Ollie?" pregunta papá.

"¡Dah! ¡Leche!", dice Ollie.

"Así es", dice papá.

Ollie escucha un sonido animal. **Toma** la mano de su padre. Caminan hacia el sonido. Llegan a una cerca. **Encuentran** una cabra. La cabra tiene cuernos clavados en la cerca. La cabra se sienta en el suelo. No se mueve. Sus cuernos están entre la madera y no puede moverse. Ollie y su padre miran a la cabra.

"Me siento tan mal por la cabra", dice Ollie. Parece triste.

"¡Pobre chico!" dice papá.

"Se ve tan triste", dice Ollie.

"Podemos ayudarlo", dice papá.

"¡Sí!" dice Ollie.

Se acercan a la cabra. Ollie está nervioso. Papá dice que no se preocupe. Los cuernos están atascados y la cabra no les hará daño. Ollie mira a los ojos de la cabra. La cabra **necesita** ayuda.

Ollie habla con la cabra. **Trata** de hacer sonidos suaves. Quiere mantener la cabra en calma.

El padre de Ollie intenta mover los cuernos. Intenta el cuerno derecho. Intenta el cuerno izquierdo. No se mueven. Después de diez minutos, se **rinden**.

"No puedo hacerlo", dice el padre de Ollie.

"¿Estás seguro?" pregunta Ollie.

"Los cuernos están atascados", dice papá.

"¿Qué hacemos?", pregunta Ollie.

El área alrededor de la cabra es barro. No hay hierba. El padre de Ollie toma un poco de hierba de la tierra y la lleva a la cabra. La cabra se come la hierba. Parece hambrienta. La hierba se ha ido. Ollie consigue más hierba para llevar a la cabra. Acarician a la cabra por unos minutos. La cabra parece agradecida.

"Vamos a decirle al dueño", dice papá.

"Sí", dice Ollie. "Quizás puedan ayudarla."

Ollie y su padre van a la taquilla. La taquilla es una pequeña estructura en la entrada. Un hombre trabaja allí. Ollie y su padre entran.

"Hola, señor", dice el padre de Ollie.

"¿Cómo puedo ayudarte?", pregunta el hombre.

"Hay una cabra-", dice el padre de Ollie.

El hombre interrumpe al padre de Ollie. Agita su mano. Se ve aburrido. "Sí, lo sabemos."

"¿Sabes lo de la cabra?" pregunta Ollie.

"¿La cabra atrapada en la cerca?" pregunta el hombre.

"¡Sí!", dicen Ollie y su papá.

"Oh sí, esa es Patty", dice el hombre. "Ella puede salir cuando quiera. Sólo le gusta la atención."

Ollie le **da** a su papá una mirada sorprendida. Ollie y su papá se ríen.

"Patty, ¡qué cabra!" dice Ollie.

69

RESUMEN

Ollie se despierta un sábado. Él y su padre deciden hacer algo divertido. Van a una granja para ver animales. Ven y tocan muchos animales: vacas, caballos, ovejas, y más. Caminan alrededor de la granja. Es un día hermoso. Encuentran una cabra atrapada en una cerca. Tratan de ayudar a la cabra. La cabra está atascada por los cuernos. Le dan de comer hierba. Ollie y su padre van a buscar ayuda. El hombre en la taquilla los escucha. Les dice que a la cabra le gusta engañar a la gente para llamar la atención. Ollie y su papá se ríen.

Lista de Vocabulario

to work	trabajar
to do	hacer
to want	querer
to go	ir
to use	utilizar
to call	llamar
to come	venir
to say	decir
to know	saber
to ask	preguntar
to think	pensar
to tell	decir
to see	ver
to become	convertir
to make	hacer

to take	tomar
to find	encontrar
to feel	sentir
to look	mirar
to get	obtener
to need	necesitar
to try	intentar
to give	dar

PREGUNTAS

1) ¿Qué deciden hacer Ollie y su padre el sábado?

    a) ir al cine

    b) ir a una granja

    c) jugar videojuegos

    d) ir a la escuela

2) ¿De qué animal sabe mucho el padre de Ollie?

    a) ovejas

    b) cerdos

    c) jirafas

    d) vacas

3) ¿Qué le pasa a la cabra?

    a) se esconde

    b) come

c) se ha atascado

d) está enojada

4) ¿Qué hacen Ollie y su padre por la cabra?

a) liberarla

b) darle hierba y acariciarla

c) llamar a la policía para conseguirlo

d) darle un beso

5) ¿Qué hace Patty?

a) deja la granja

b) ella come basura

c) va a la taquilla

d) actúa que está atascada para llamar la atención

RESPUESTAS

1) ¿Qué deciden hacer Ollie y su padre el sábado?

   b) ir a una granja

2) ¿De qué animal sabe mucho el padre de Ollie?

   a) ovejas

3) ¿Qué le pasa a la cabra?

   c) se ha atascado

4) ¿Qué hacen Ollie y su padre por la cabra?

   b) darle hierba y acariciarla

5) ¿Qué hace Patty?

   d) actúa que está atascada para llamar la atención

Translation of the Story

The Goat

Ollie wakes up. The sun is shining. He remembers: it is Saturday. Today his dad does not **work**. That means Ollie and his dad **do** something together. What can they do? Ollie **wants** to go to the movies. He also wants to play video games.

Ollie is twelve years old. He goes to school. Saturday he does not go to school. He **uses** Saturday to do what he wants. His dad lets him decide. So Ollie wants to do something fun.

"Daaaaaad!" **calls** Ollie. "**Come** here!"

Ollie waits.

His dad enters Ollie's bedroom.

"Today is Saturday," **says** Ollie.

"I **know**, son," says Ollie's dad.

"I want to do something fun!" says Ollie.

"Me too," says Dad.

"What can we do?" **asks** Ollie.

"What do you want to do?" asks his dad.

"Go to the movies," says Ollie.

"We always go to the movies on Saturday," says Ollie's dad.

"Play video games," says Ollie.

"We play video games everyday!" says Dad.

"Ok, ok," says Ollie. He **thinks**. He remembers his teacher at school. His teacher **tells** the students to go outside. The teacher tells them the fresh air is good. At school, they study animals. Ollie learns about animals in the jungle, animals in the ocean, and animals on farms.

That's it!

"Dad, let's go to a farm!" says Ollie. Ollie's dad thinks that is a great idea. He has always wanted to **see** and touch farm animals.

They take the car. Ollie's dad drives to the countryside. They see a sign that says "Animal Farm". They follow the signs and park the car.

Ollie and his dad buy tickets to enter. Tickets cost $5. They leave the ticket office. There is a big wooden building, the farmhouse. Behind the farmhouse, there is a huge field. The field has trees, grass, and fences. In each fence is a different type of animal. There are hundreds of animals.

Ollie is excited. He sees chickens, horses, ducks, and pigs. He touches them and listens to them. Ollie **makes** a sound to each animal. To the ducks, he says "quack". To the pigs, he says "oink". To the horses, he says "nay". To the chickens, he says "bok bok". The animals stare at Ollie.

Past the animals in cages, Ollie sees a flock of sheep. Ollie's dad tells him that female sheep are called ewes. Male sheep are rams. Baby sheep are called lambs. The sheep are eating grass.

"They can see us," says Dad.

"But they are not looking at us," says Ollie.

"Sheep can see behind themselves. They don't have to turn their heads," says Dad. Ollie's dad knows a lot about sheep.

"They cut the hair on the sheep in spring," says Dad. He tells Ollie how the sheep's wool **becomes** sweaters, scarves and other warm clothing. Ollie has a sweater made of wool. It is warm.

Ollie and his dad walk around the field. The grass is green. There are cows in a corner. One of the mother cows feeds a baby calf.

"You know what cows make, Ollie?" asks Dad.

"Duh! Milk!" says Ollie.

"That's right," says Dad.

Ollie hears an animal sound. He **takes** his dad's hand. They walk towards the sound. They come to a fence. They **find** a goat. The goat has horns stuck in the fence. The goat sits on the ground. It does not move. Its horns are between the wood and it can't move. Ollie and his dad **look** at the goat.

"I feel so bad for the goat," says Ollie. She seems sad.

"Poor guy!" says Dad.

"He looks so sad," says Ollie.

"We can help him," Dad says.

"Yeah!" says Ollie.

They get close to the goat. Ollie is nervous. Dad says not to worry. The horns are stuck and the goat will not hurt them. Ollie looks into the eyes of the goat. The goat **needs** help. Ollie talks to the goat. He **tries** to make soft sounds. He wants to keep the goat calm.

Ollie's dad tries to move the horns. He tries the right horn. He tries the left horn. They don't move. After ten minutes, they **give up**.

"I can't do it," says Ollie's dad.

"Are you sure?" asks Ollie.

"The horns are stuck," says Dad.

"What do we do?" asks Ollie.

The area around the goat is mud. There is no grass left. Ollie's dad takes some grass from the ground and brings it to the goat. The goat eats the grass. The goat looks hungry. The grass is gone. Ollie gets more grass to take to the goat. They pet the goat for a few minutes. The goat seems grateful.

"Let's tell the owner," says Dad.

"Yeah," says Ollie. "Maybe they can help her."

Ollie and his dad go to the ticket office. The ticket office is a small building at the entrance. A man works there. Ollie and his dad go inside.

"Hello, sir," says Ollie's dad.

"How can I help you?" asks the man.

"There's a goat—" says Ollie's dad.

The man interrupts Ollie's dad. He waves his hand. He looks bored. "Yeah, we know."

"You know about the goat?" asks Ollie.

"The goat stuck in the fence?" asks the man.

"Yes!" say Ollie and his dad.

"Oh yes, that's Patty," says the man. "She can get herself out whenever she wants. She just likes the attention."

Ollie **gives** his dad a surprised look. Ollie and his dad laugh.

"Patty, what a goat!" Ollie says.

CONCLUSION

You did it!

Y ou finished a whole book in a brand new language. That in and of itself is quite the accomplishment, isn't it?

Congratulate yourself on time well spent and a job well done. Now that you've finished the book, you have familiarized yourself with over 500 new vocabulary words, comprehended the heart of 3 short stories, and listened to loads of dialogue unfold, all without going anywhere!

Charlemagne said "To have another language is to possess a second soul." After immersing yourself in this book, you are broadening your horizons and opening a whole new path for yourself.

http://www.LearnLikeNatives.com
www.LearnLikeNatives.com

Have you thought about how much you know now that you did not know before? You've learned everything from how to greet and how to express your emotions to basics like colors and place words. You can tell time and ask question. All without opening a schoolbook. Instead, you've cruised through fun, interesting stories and possibly listened to them as well.

Perhaps before you weren't able to distinguish meaning when you listened to Spanish. If you used the audiobook, we bet you can now pick out meanings and words when you hear someone speaking. Regardless, we are sure you have taken an important step to being more fluent. You are well on your way!

Best of all, you have made the essential step of distinguishing in your mind the idea that most often hinders people studying a new language. By approaching Spanish through our short stories and dialogs, instead of formal lessons with just grammar and vocabulary, you are no longer in the 'learning' mindset. Your approach is much more similar to an osmosis, focused on speaking and using the language, which is the end goal, after all!

So, what's next?

This is just the first of five books, all packed full of short stories and dialogs, covering essential, everyday Spanish that will ensure you master the basics. You can find the rest of the books in the series, as well as a whole host of other resources, at **LearnLikeNatives.com**. Simply add the book to your library to take the next step in your language learning journey. If you are ever in need of new ideas or direction, refer to our 'Speak Like a Native' eBook, available to you for free at LearnLikeNatives.com, which clearly outlines practical steps you can take to continue learning any language you choose.

We also encourage you to get out into the real world and practice your Spanish. You have a leg up on most beginners, after all—instead of pure textbook learning, you have been absorbing the sound and soul of the language. Do not underestimate the foundation you have built reviewing the chapters of this book. Remember, no one feels 100% confident when they speak with a native speaker in another language.

One of the coolest things about being human is connecting with others. Communicating with someone in their own language is a wonderful gift. Knowing the language turns you into a local and opens up your world. You will see the reward of learning languages for many years to come, so keep that practice up!. Don't let your fears stop you from taking the chance to use your Spanish. Just give it a try, and remember that you will make mistakes. However, these mistakes will teach you so much, so view every single one as a small victory! Learning is growth.

Don't let the quest for learning end here! There is so much you can do to continue the learning process in an organic way, like you did with this book. Add another book from Learn Like a Native to your library. Listen to Spanish talk radio. Watch some of the great Spanish films. Put on the latest

CD from Rosalia. Take salsa lessons in Spanish. Whatever you do, don't stop because every little

step you take counts towards learning a new language, culture, and way of communicating.

www.LearnLikeNatives.com

Learn Like a Native is a revolutionary **language education brand** that is taking the linguistic world by storm. Forget boring grammar books that never get you anywhere, Learn Like a Native teaches you languages in a fast and fun way that actually works!

As an international, multichannel, language learning platform, we provide **books, audio guides and eBooks** so that you can acquire the knowledge you need, swiftly and easily.

Our **subject-based learning**, structured around real-world scenarios, builds your conversational muscle and ensures you learn the content most relevant to your requirements. Discover our tools at ***LearnLikeNatives.com***.

When it comes to learning languages, we've got you covered!

Lightning Source UK Ltd.
Milton Keynes UK
UKHW020627160822
407367UK00001B/39